REALLY WEIRD ANIMALS

SNAKES AND LIZARDS

CLARE HIBBERT

First published in paperback in 2015

First published in 2011 by Franklin Watts

Copyright © Arcturus Holdings Limited

Franklin Watts
338 Euston Road
London NW1 3BH

Franklin Watts Australia
Level 17/207 Kent Street, Sydney NSW 2000

Produced by Arcturus Publishing Limited,
26/27 Bickels Yard, 151–153 Bermondsey Street, London SE1 3HA

Series concept: Discovery Books Ltd, 2 College Street, Ludlow, Shropshire SY8 1AN
www.discoverybooks.net

Managing editor: Paul Humphrey
Editor and picture researcher: Clare Hibbert
Design: sprout.uk.com

Photo acknowledgements: Corbis: cover and pp 1 (DLILLC), 15 (Paul A Souders); FLPA: pp 9 (Chris Mattison), 10 (Michael & Patricia Fogden/Minden Pictures), 16t (Michael & Patricia Fogden/ Minden Pictures), 17b (Michael & Patricia Fogden/Minden Pictures), 20b (Edward Myles), 21 (Michael & Patricia Fogden/Minden Pictures), 22t (Thomas Marent/Minden Pictures), 23b (Thomas Marent/Minden Pictures), 28l (Patricio Robles Gil/Minden Pictures); iStockphoto: pp 3 (Snowleopard1), 4t (waikiki), 5t (larus_ov), 7b (iSailorr), 8b (Snowleopard1), 14b (JJMaree), 16b (Snowleopard1), 17t (Snowleopard1), 18t (AYImages), 19t (miralex), 19b (cotesebastien), 20t (PaulTessier), 23t (doucettej), 24b (drop-off-dean), 26t (benjamint444), 31 (PaulTessier); NHPA: pp 6t (Stephen Dalton), 12l (Cede Prudente), 13 (Stephen Dalton), 14t (Anthony Bannister), 25t (John Cancalosi), 27 (Anthony Bannister); Photolibrary: p 22b (Paul Freed); Shutterstock: pp 4b (Sebastian Duda), 5b (Eduard Kyslynskyy), 6b (Eduardo Rivero), 7t (Peter Wollinga), 8t (Alex Edmonds), 11l (BMCL), 11r (kkaplin), 12r (Lawrence Wee), 18b (kkaplin), 24t (Eric Isselée), 25b (fivespots), 26b (Ashley Whitworth), 28b (Casey K Bishop), 29l (Crok Photography), 29r (oariff), 32 (Eduardo Rivero).

Cover picture: A Jackson's chameleon, East Africa.

A CIP catalogue record for this book is available from the British Library.

Dewey Decimal Classification Number 597.9'6

ISBN 978 1 4451 3819 0
SL001750UK

Printed in China

Franklin Watts is a division of Hachette Children's Books, an Hachette UK company.
www.hachette.co.uk

CONTENTS

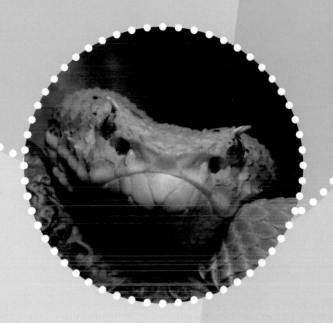

Chameleon **4**

Basilisk Lizard **6**

Vine Snake **8**

Leaf-Nosed Snake **9**

Frilled Lizard **10**

Paradise Flying Snake **12**

Draco Lizard **13**

Armadillo Lizard **14**

Thorny Devil **15**

Eyelash Viper **16**

Komodo Dragon **18**

Iguana **19**

African Rock Python **20**

Egg-Eating Snake **21**

Leaf-Tailed Gecko **22**

Tokay Gecko **24**

Gila Monster **25**

Blue-Tongued Skink **26**

Spitting Cobra **27**

Sidewinder **28**

King Cobra **29**

Glossary **30**

Further Information **31**

Index **32**

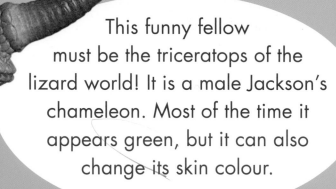

This funny fellow must be the triceratops of the lizard world! It is a male Jackson's chameleon. Most of the time it appears green, but it can also change its skin colour.

CHAMELEON

CHAMELEON FACTS

SIZE: 3-68 cm long, depending on species
HOME: Africa, southern Europe, parts of Asia
EATS: insects

Chameleons change colour to blend in with their surroundings – or simply to show their mood or health.

This colourful customer is a panther chameleon. Its curled-up tail is brilliant at gripping – it acts as a fifth limb.

WEIRD OR WHAT?

A chameleon can rotate and focus each eye separately. This gives it excellent all-round vision for pinpointing the position of prey.

Chameleons eat locusts and other insect prey. They shoot their long, sticky tongues out and in again too fast for the human eye to see.

BASILISK LIZARD

Basilisk lizards live beside rainforest streams, and can race across the surface of the water to escape danger. They can cross a 3-metre stream in just 2 seconds.

These lizards are sometimes nicknamed Jesus Christ lizards, after the Bible story where Jesus walks across the Sea of Galilee.

WEIRD OR WHAT?

Basilisk lizards are good swimmers. They can stay underwater for up to half an hour.

Basilisks often have speckles or stripes on their greeny-brown skin. This patterning provides excellent camouflage in their forest home.

BASILISK LIZARD FACTS

SIZE: up to 1 m long
HOME: rainforests, Central
and South America
EATS: insects, fruit, flowers,
fish, snakes, birds,
eggs, rodents

Basilisk lizards have
a lightweight, skinny body and a
long, whip-like tail. Some have a sail,
like the dinosaur Spinosaurus, along
their back and tail.

The basilisk is named after
a mythical monster that was
half-cockerel, half-snake. Its crest
looks a bit like a cock's comb.

How many snakes can you spot? Vine snakes have amazing camouflage.

VINE SNAKE FACTS

SIZE: 75 cm to 1.5 m long
HOME: rainforests, dry forests, grasslands, Americas, Asia, Africa
EATS: lizards, frogs, rodents, birds

VINE SNAKE

WEIRD OR WHAT?

Some vine snakes have a trick for scaring off predators. They puff out their necks to reveal a bright colour on the skin between their scales.

Asian vine snakes hunt by day. They have unusual, keyhole-shaped pupils and excellent binocular vision.

LEAF-NOSED SNAKE

There are no prizes for guessing how the leaf-nosed snake got its name. The female has a frilly-edged, leaf-shaped snout!

WEIRD OR WHAT?

A male leaf-nosed snake looks very different to its mate. Its snout ends in a sharp point. No wonder the male is nicknamed the spear-nosed snake!

Leaf-nosed snakes slip through the trees, hunting lizards. Sometimes they nuzzle their prey with their snouts. Experts think this helps them know exactly where to strike.

LEAF-NOSED SNAKE FACTS

SIZE: about 50 cm long
HOME: rainforests, dry forests, Madagascar
EATS: small lizards (geckos, anoles)

FRILLED LIZARD

FRILLED LIZARD FACTS

FRILLED LIZARD FACTS

SIZE: 1 m long
HOME: rainforests, Australasia
EATS: mostly insects, also spiders,
      lizards, small mammals

'Look how big and scary I am!' this lizard seems to be saying. The frilled lizard has a flap of skin around its neck that makes it look much larger than it really is.

The lizard sticks out the frill by opening its mouth wide. It makes a loud hissing noise at the same time.

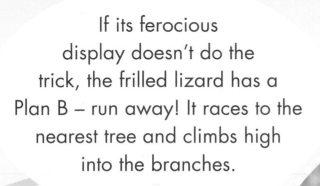

If its ferocious display doesn't do the trick, the frilled lizard has a Plan B – run away! It races to the nearest tree and climbs high into the branches.

Male frilled lizards also use their neck frill to scare off rivals. They fight over females at the start of the breeding season.

WEIRD OR WHAT?

Frilled lizards lay their eggs just under the soil. The sex of the babies depends on the weather - in hot conditions, all the babies will be female.

PARADISE FLYING SNAKE

WEIRD OR WHAT?

Flying snakes can glide as far as 100 metres.

Is it a bird? Is it a plane? No, it's a snake! A paradise flying snake cannot really fly, but it can glide. It launches its body from the top of a tree.

FLYING SNAKE FACTS

SIZE: up to 1.2 m long
HOME: mangrove forests, rainforests, South-East Asia
EATS: lizards, frogs, birds, bats

The paradise flying snake spends its life in the trees. Its favourite hang-out is the coconut palm.

Snakes aren't the only reptiles that have evolved the ability to 'fly'. The draco lizard can glide for distances of 50 metres.

WEIRD OR WHAT?

'Draco' means dragon. This little lizard's nickname is 'flying dragon'.

The draco has scale-covered flaps of skin between its front and back legs that act like wings.

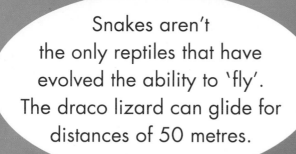

DRACO LIZARD FACTS

SIZE: around 20 cm long
HOME: rainforests, South-East Asia
EATS: insects

ARMADILLO LIZARD

WEIRD OR WHAT?

Very few lizards feed their young, but armadillo lizard mums do.

The armadillo lizard has a clever defence. It curls up into a ball, tucking its tail into its mouth. No predator would want to take on that spiky meal!

ARMADILLO LIZARD FACTS

SIZE: 25 cm long
HOME: deserts, Africa
EATS: insects (especially termites), spiders

In the wild, the armadillo lizard lives in dry, desert areas. It's also a popular pet.

THORNY DEVIL

Here's another prickly customer! The well-named thorny devil is covered in sharp spines as a defence against predators.

WEIRD OR WHAT?

A thorny devil can eat thousands of ants in a single day.

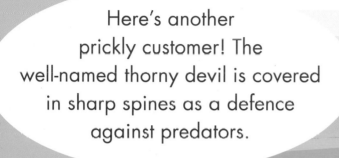

THORNY DEVIL FACTS

SIZE: up to 20 cm long
HOME: deserts, Australia
EATS: ants

With its yellow scales, the eyelash viper blends in perfectly with its fruity hiding place – a palm laden with juicy dates.

EYELASH VIPER FACTS

SIZE: around 75 cm long
HOME: rainforests, Central and South America
EATS: frogs, lizards, birds, rodents

EYELASH VIPER

Like all pit vipers, the eyelash viper has a heat-sensitive pit on each side of its head. These pits allow the snake to locate prey by body heat.

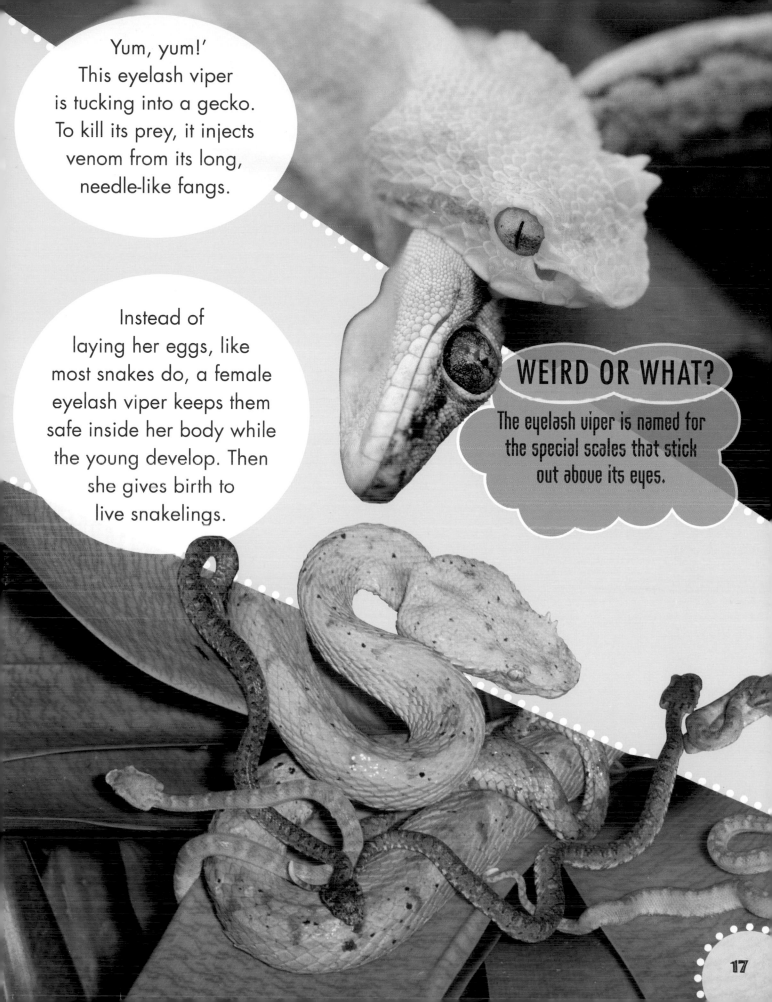

Yum, yum!'
This eyelash viper
is tucking into a gecko.
To kill its prey, it injects
venom from its long,
needle-like fangs.

Instead of
laying her eggs, like
most snakes do, a female
eyelash viper keeps them
safe inside her body while
the young develop. Then
she gives birth to
live snakelings.

WEIRD OR WHAT?

The eyelash viper is named for
the special scales that stick
out above its eyes.

WEIRD OR WHAT?

Komodo dragons are the world's largest lizards.

This lizard might look comical – but its bite is no laughing matter. The komodo dragon has a venomous bite to paralyze prey.

KOMODO DRAGON

Komodo dragons prefer carrion. These ones are tucking into a dead water buffalo. They eat their meal whole, then cough up the horns, hair and teeth in a pellet.

KOMODO DRAGON FACTS

SIZE: 2-3 m long
HOME: Indonesia
EATS: carrion, mammals, invertebrates, reptiles, birds, eggs

This colourful character is a green iguana. Special bacteria in its gut help it to digest plant foods such as buds, flowers, fruit and leaves.

WEIRD OR WHAT?

The marine iguana can dive to depths of 10 metres.

IGUANA

IGUANA FACTS

SIZE: more than 1.5 m long
HOME: Central and South America
EATS: plants, algae

This marine iguana lives in the Galapagos Islands. It basks on the rocks, but feeds in the sea, nibbling algae off underwater rocks.

AFRICAN ROCK PYTHON

Open wide! Like many snakes, the African rock python can open up its lower jaw to swallow prey larger than its own head. This one is eating an antelope.

AFRICAN ROCK PYTHON FACTS

SIZE: around 5 m long
HOME: grasslands, sub-Saharan Africa
EATS: rodents, goats, gazelles, warthogs, crocodiles

Pythons kill their prey by constriction – coiling their body tighter and tighter around the victim. The victim dies of a heart attack or suffocates.

EGG-EATING SNAKE

This nest raider is an egg-eating snake. It climbs trees in search of birds' nests, where it will swallow an egg, shell and all.

WEIRD OR WHAT?

Egg-eating snakes can tell by sniffing whether an egg is fresh or not. It won't eat rotten eggs.

EGG-EATING SNAKE FACTS

SIZE: about 75 cm long
HOME: grasslands, forests, Africa
EATS: birds' eggs

The egg-eating snake doesn't have teeth. Spines inside its throat pierce the shell. Then the snake swallows the egg yolk and white and spits out the shell.

This little lizard is a true master of disguise. With its curled-up brown body, the fantastic leaf-tailed gecko looks just like a dead leaf!

Leaf-Tailed Gecko

Fantastic leaf-tailed geckos live on the island of Madagascar. They rely on their cunning camouflage to escape the attention of predators. Can you spot the one in the leaves?

The mossy leaf-tailed gecko goes one better. Like many chameleons, it can change the colour of its skin. This one is blending in with the bark of a tree.

WEIRD OR WHAT?

The spearpoint leaf-tailed gecko is the smallest species. It would fit comfortably in the palm of your hand.

Mossy leaf-tailed geckos also colour themselves to match moss and lichen.

LEAF-TAILED GECKO FACTS

SIZE: 7.5–30 cm long
HOME: rainforests, dry forests, Madagascar
EATS: insects, spiders, snails

Tokay Gecko

All geckos chirp to attract a mate, but the tokay gecko is the noisiest. Its name mimics the sound of its loud, croaky call.

TOKAY GECKO FACTS

SIZE: about 35 cm long
HOME: rainforests, South-East Asia
EATS: insects

Like many geckos, the tokay gecko has no eyelids. It licks its eyes to stop them drying out in the sun.

WEIRD OR WHAT?

Many tokay geckos now live in cities. Instead of climbing trees for their insect prey, they climb people's walls and ceilings.

Chomp! Chomp! This gila monster's munching a deer mouse.

GILA MONSTER FACTS

SIZE: 60 cm long
HOME: deserts, south-western United States, north-western Mexico
EATS: eggs, chicks, small mammals

GILA MONSTER

The gila monster has a keen sense of smell for tracking down prey. Like all lizards and snakes, it flicks its tongue to detect chemicals in the air.

WEIRD OR WHAT?

The gila monster has a venomous bite. Rather than being injected, the venom oozes out of grooves on some of the bottom teeth.

BLUE-TONGUED SKINK

WEIRD OR WHAT?

Like many lizards, skinks can lose their tails, leaving them wiggling to distract a predator while they make a quick getaway.

Doesn't this lizard know that it's rude to pull tongues? The blue-tongued skink sticks out its tongue to surprise predators.

BLUE-TONGUED SKINK FACTS

SIZE: up to 60 cm long
HOME: various habitats, Australia
EATS: insects, spiders, fruit, slugs, snails

The skink's tail confuses eagles and other birds of prey swooping from above. Its stumpy shape makes it hard to distinguish from the skink's head.

SPITTING COBRA

The spitting cobra defends itself from bigger hunters by 'spitting'. It squirts a jet of venom from its fangs directly at an attacker's eyes. The venom can cause blindness.

WEIRD OR WHAT?

A spitting cobra can 'spit' its venom as far as 2 metres.

Despite their brilliant defence, spitting cobras are still preyed upon. Their main enemies are secretary birds and banded mongooses.

SPITTING COBRA FACTS

SIZE: usually 120-220 cm long
HOME: sub-Saharan Africa
EATS: small mammals, frogs, lizards, snakes

SIDEWINDER

The sidewinder, or horned rattlesnake, is named for the way it moves across the desert. It throws its body forwards, this way and that, leaving behind distinctive marks in the sand.

WEIRD OR WHAT?

Young sidewinders use their tail as a lure to tempt lizard prey to come near.

The sidewinder's sandy colouring provides excellent camouflage.

SIDEWINDER FACTS

SIZE: 75 cm long
HOME: deserts, North America
EATS: lizards, rodents

KING COBRA

WEIRD OR WHAT?

The king cobra is the world's longest venomous snake.

The venomous king cobra is an aggressive, fast-moving hunter. It spreads out its neck or hood to appear more threatening. It preys on other snakes.

Many snake charmers perform with king cobras. They play a flute while the snake sways in time with the music.

KING COBRA FACTS

SIZE: more than 5.5 m
HOME: forests, South-East Asia
EATS: snakes, lizards, birds, small mammals

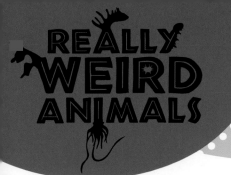
alga (plural algae) One of a group of living things that include seaweeds and some plankton.

bacterium (plural bacteria) One of a group of tiny, one-celled living things. Some bacteria cause disease, but others are useful, for example by helping to break down food during digestion.

bask To sunbathe. Reptiles cannot produce their own body heat. They warm up by sitting in the sun.

binocular vision A way of seeing that combines the view from two eyes at once. Tiny differences between the two images make it possible to judge distances accurately.

breeding season The time of year when animals come together to mate and produce young.

camouflage Colours or patterns that help an animal to blend in to the surrounding environment to avoid being seen by predators, prey or both.

carrion The rotting flesh of a dead animal.

constriction The killing method used by some snakes, including pythons and boa constrictors, which involves coiling tighter and tighter around prey and squeezing.

digest Break down food in the body.

focus To adjust the eye in order to see a clear image.

invertebrate An animal that has no backbone. Insects and spiders are invertebrates.

limb The arm or leg of an animal.

lure Something that is used to tempt – for example to bring prey animals near.

mammal A warm-blooded animal with a backbone. Mammals have fur and feed their young on mother's milk.

mangrove A tree that has adapted to living in the salty water of tropical coastal swamps.

neck frill A flap of skin that extends around the head, making an animal appear larger.

paralyze To make something unable to move.

pellet A lump of undigested matter that some animals spit up after a meal.

predator An animal that hunts and kills other animals for food.

prey An animal that is hunted and killed by another animal for food.

pupil The area through which light enters the eye.

rainforest A forest habitat where rain falls almost every day. In a tropical rainforest, the climate is hot and steamy all year round.

reptile A cold-blooded animal with a backbone. Reptiles have scales and usually lay eggs on land (though some give birth to live young).

rotate To turn in a circle around a central point.

scale One of the thin, flat plates that cover the skin of a snake or lizard.

species One particular type of living thing. Members of the same species look similar and can reproduce together in the wild.

suffocate To stop breathing, for example because the chest and lungs are too squashed to take in air.

tropical Describes the warm part of the world near to the equator (the imaginary line that circles the middle of the earth).

venom A chemical that is injected into another animal to paralyze it.

FURTHER INFORMATION

Books

Insiders: Reptiles by Mark Hutchinson (Templar Publishing, 2009)

Lizards: Weird and Wonderful by Margery Facklam (Little, Brown and Company, 2003)

Snake by Chris Mattison (Dorling Kindersley, 2006)

Usborne Discovery: Snakes by Rachel Firth (Usborne, 2008)

Weird Wildlife: Reptiles by Jen Green (Belitha, 2003)

DVDs

David Attenborough's Life in Cold Blood (2 Entertain Video, 2008)

National Geographic: Reptiles (National Geographic, 2010)

Websites

BBC Wildlife Finder
www.bbc.co.uk/nature/life/Reptile

Kids Konnect: Lizards
http://www.kidskonnect.com/subject-index/13-animals/41-lizards.html

National Geographic: Reptiles
http://animals.nationalgeographic.com/animals/reptiles/

Natural History Museum: Chameleons
http://www.nhm.ac.uk/kids-only//life/life-disguise/chameleon/

African rock pythons 20
algae 19
armadillo lizards 14

bacteria 19
basilisk lizards 6–7
basking 19
binocular vision 8
blue-tongued skinks 26
breeding 11

camouflage 4, 6, 8, 16, 22, 23, 28
carrion 18
chameleons 4–5
cobras 27, 29
constriction 20

defences 8, 14, 15, 26, 27
deserts 14, 15, 25, 28
digestion 19
draco lizards 13

egg-eating snakes 21
eggs 11, 17, 20
  as food 7, 18, 21, 25
eyelash vipers 16–17
eyes 5, 8, 17, 24, 27

flying snakes 12
frilled lizards 10–11

geckos 22–24
gila monsters 25
gliding 12, 13
grasslands 8, 20, 21

iguanas 19

king cobras 29
komodo dragons 18

leaf-nosed snakes 9
leaf-tailed geckos 22–23
lures 28

mangroves 12
marine iguanas 19

neck frills 10, 11

pellets 18
predators 8, 14, 15, 22, 26
prey 5, 9, 16, 17, 18, 20, 24, 25, 28

rainforests 6, 7, 8, 9, 10, 12, 13, 16, 23, 24

scales 8, 13, 16, 17
sidewinders 28
snake charmers 29
spitting cobras 27
suffocation 20

thorny devils 15
tokay geckos 24

venom 17, 18, 25, 27, 29
vine snakes 8